# A TALE OF TWO CITIES

The year is 1775, and in a room above a wine shop in Paris sits a white-haired man, busy making shoes. For eighteen years he was a prisoner in the Bastille. Now he is a free man, but he does not know his name or recognize his friends. He knows only that he must go on making shoes.

In a coach driving into Paris sits Lucie, the daughter he has never seen. Lucie takes her father back to London and with her love and care, he forgets the past and learns to live again as a free man.

But in the stormy years of the French Revolution, the past is neither dead, nor forgotten. And soon its dangerous secrets pull Lucie and the people she loves back to Paris ... where that terrible machine of death, the Guillotine, waits hungrily for the enemies of France.

OXFORD BOOKWORMS LIBRARY
*Classics*

# A Tale of Two Cities
Stage 4 (1400 headwords)

Series Editor: Jennifer Bassett
Founder Editor: Tricia Hedge
Activities Editors: Jennifer Bassett and Alison Baxter

American Edition: Daphne Mackey, University of Washington

CHARLES DICKENS

# A Tale of Two Cities

*Retold by*
Ralph Mowat

OXFORD UNIVERSITY PRESS

# OXFORD

UNIVERSITY PRESS

Great Clarendon Street, Oxford OX2 6DP

Oxford University Press is a department of the University of Oxford.
It furthers the University's objective of excellence in research, scholarship,
and education by publishing worldwide in

Oxford New York

Auckland Cape Town Dar es Salaam Hong Kong Karachi
Kuala Lumpur Madrid Melbourne Mexico City Nairobi
New Delhi Shanghai Taipei Toronto

With offices in

Argentina Austria Brazil Chile Czech Republic France Greece
Guatemala Hungary Italy Japan Poland Portugal Singapore
South Korea Switzerland Thailand Turkey Ukraine Vietnam

OXFORD and OXFORD ENGLISH are registered trade marks of
Oxford University Press in the UK and in certain other countries

ISBN 978 0 19 423759 8

Printed in China

*Illustrated by:* Mark Hargreaves

# CONTENTS

# I

## The Road to Paris—1775

It was the best of times, it was the worst of times. It was the season of light, it was the season of darkness. It was the spring of hope, it was the winter of sadness. It was the year one thousand seven hundred and seventy-five.

In France there was a King and a Queen, and in England there was a King and a Queen. They believed that nothing would ever change. But in France things were bad and getting worse. The people were poor, hungry, and unhappy. The King made paper money and spent it, and the people had nothing to eat. Behind closed doors in the homes of the people, voices spoke in whispers against the King and his noblemen; they were only whispers, but they were the angry whispers of desperate people.

Late one November night, in that same year, 1775, a coach going from London to Dover stopped at the top of a long hill. The horses were tired, but as they rested, the driver heard

1

another horse coming fast up the hill behind them. The rider stopped his horse beside the coach and shouted:

"I want a passenger, Mr. Jarvis Lorry, from Tellson's Bank in London."

"I am Mr. Jarvis Lorry," said one of the passengers, putting his head out of the window. "What do you want?"

"It's me! Jerry, Jerry Cruncher, from Tellson's Bank, sir," cried the man on the horse.

"What's the matter, Jerry?" called Mr. Lorry.

"A message for you, Mr. Lorry. You've got to wait at Dover for a young lady."

"Very well, Jerry," said Mr. Lorry. "Tell them my answer is—CAME BACK TO LIFE."

It was a strange message, and a stranger answer. No one in the coach understood what they meant.

The next day Mr. Lorry was sitting in his hotel in Dover when a young lady arrived. She was pretty, with golden hair and blue eyes, and Mr. Lorry remembered a small child, almost a baby. He had carried her in his arms when he came from Calais to Dover, from France to England, many years ago. Mr. Lorry asked the young lady to sit down.

"Miss Manette," he said. "I have a strange story to tell you, about one of the customers of Tellson's Bank. That's where I work."

"Yes, but I don't quite understand, Mr. Lorry," said the young lady. "I received a message from Tellson's Bank, asking me to come here to meet you. I understood there was some news about my poor father's money. He died so long ago—before I was born. What is this story you want to tell me?"

"About twenty years ago, Miss Manette, a French doctor married an English lady. They had a daughter, but just before she was born, her father disappeared. Nobody knew what had happened to him. Not long afterwards his unhappy wife died, and their daughter was brought back to England."

"But this is like my father's story, Mr. Lorry. And wasn't it you who brought me back to England?"

"Yes, that's true, Miss Manette. Many years ago I brought you from France to England, and Tellson's Bank has taken care of you since then. You were told that your father had died. But think, Miss Manette. Perhaps your father wasn't dead. Perhaps he was in prison. Not because he had done something

*"What is this story you want to tell me?"*

wrong! But just because he had a powerful enemy—an enemy with the power to send him to prison and to keep him there, hidden and forgotten, for eighteen years!"

"Can it be true? Is it possible that my father is still alive?" Lucie Manette stared at Mr. Lorry. Her face was white, and her hands trembled. "It will be his ghost—not him!"

"No, Miss Manette," said Mr. Lorry gently. "He is alive, but he has changed a lot. Even his name had been forgotten! And we must ask no questions about the past, no questions at all. It would be too dangerous. He has been taken to the house of an old servant in Paris, and we are going there to bring him back to life."

# 2

## A Wine Shop in Paris

In the part of Paris called Saint Antoine everyone was poor. The streets were narrow and dirty, and the food shops were almost empty. The faces of the children looked old already because they were so hungry. In the wine shop of Monsieur Defarge there were not many customers, and Defarge was outside, talking to a man in the street. His wife, Madame Defarge, sat inside the shop, knitting and watching. Defarge came in and his wife looked at him, then turned her eyes to look at two new customers, a man of about sixty and a young lady. Defarge went over to speak to them, suddenly kissed the young lady's hand, and led them out of the back of the shop.

4

*Madame Defarge sat inside the wine shop,
knitting and watching.*

They followed him upstairs, many stairs, until they reached
the top. Defarge took a key out of his pocket.

"Why is the door locked?" asked Mr. Lorry in surprise. "He
is a free man now."

"Because he has lived too long behind a locked door,"
replied Defarge angrily. "He is afraid if the door is not locked!

That is one of the things they have done to him."

"I'm afraid, too," whispered Miss Manette. Her blue eyes looked worriedly at Mr. Lorry. "I am afraid of him—of my father."

Defarge made a lot of noise as he opened the door. Mr. Lorry and Lucie went into the room behind him. A thin, white-haired man was sitting on a wooden seat. He was very busy, making shoes.

"Good day," said Defarge. "You are still working hard, I see."

After a while they heard a whisper. "Yes, I am still working."

"Come," said Defarge. "You have a visitor. Tell him your name."

"My name?" came the whisper. "One Hundred and Five, North Tower."

Mr. Lorry moved closer to the old man. "Dr. Manette, don't you remember me, Jarvis Lorry?" he asked gently.

The old prisoner looked up at Mr. Lorry, but there was no surprise, no understanding in his tired face, and he went back to work making shoes.

Slowly Lucie came near to the old man. After a while he noticed her.

"Who are you?" he asked.

Lucie put her arms around the old man and held him, tears of happiness and sadness running down her face. From a little bag the old man took some golden hair. He looked at it, and then he looked at Lucie's hair. "It is the same. How can it be?" He stared into Lucie's face. "No, no, you are too young, too young."

*Lucie put her arms around the old man and held him.*

Through her tears Lucie tried to explain that she was the daughter he had never seen. The old man still did not understand, but he seemed to like the sound of Lucie's voice and the touch of her warm young hand on his.

Then Lucie said to Mr. Lorry, "I think we should leave Paris at once. Can you arrange it?"

"Yes, of course," said Mr. Lorry. "But do you think he is able to travel?"

"He will be better far away from this city where he has lost so much of his life," said Lucie.

"You are right," said Defarge. "And there are many other reasons why Dr. Manette should leave France now." *Why?*

While Mr. Lorry and Defarge went to arrange for a coach to take them out of Paris, Lucie sat with her father. Exhausted by the meeting, he fell asleep on the floor, and his daughter watched him quietly and patiently until it was time to go.

When Mr. Lorry returned, he and Defarge brought food and clothes for Dr. Manette. The Doctor did everything they told him to do; he had been used to obeying orders for many years. As he came down the stairs, Mr. Lorry heard him say again and again, "One Hundred and Five, North Tower."

When they went to the coach, only one person saw them go: Madame Defarge. She stood in the doorway, and knitted and watched, seeing everything ... and seeing nothing.

# 3

## A Trial in London—1780

Tellson's Bank in the City of London was an old, dark, and ugly building. It smelled of dust and old papers, and the people who worked there all seemed old and dusty, too. Outside the building sat Jerry Cruncher, who carried messages for people in the bank.

One morning in March 1780, Jerry had to go to the Old Bailey to collect an important message from Mr. Lorry. Trials at the Old Bailey were usually for very dangerous criminals, and the prisoner that morning was a young man of about twenty-five, well dressed and quite calm.

"What's he done?" Jerry asked the doorman quietly.

"He's a spy! A French spy!" the doorman told him. "He

travels from England to France and tells the French King secret information about our English army."

"What'll happen if he's guilty?" asked Jerry.

"Oh, he'll have to die, no question of that," replied the doorman enthusiastically. "They'll hang him."

"What's his name?"

"Darnay, Charles Darnay. Not an English name, is it?"

While Jerry waited, he looked around at the crowd inside the Old Bailey and noticed a young lady of about twenty years and her father, a gentleman with very white hair. The young lady seemed very sad when she looked at the prisoner, and she held herself close to her father.

Then the trial began, and the first person who spoke against Charles Darnay was called John Barsad.

He was an honest man, he said, and proud to be an Englishman. Yes, he was, or had been, a friend of the prisoner's. And in the prisoner's pockets he had seen important plans and lists about the English armies. No, of course he had not put the lists there himself. And no, he was not a spy himself—he was not someone paid to make traps for innocent people.

Next the young lady spoke. She said that she had met the prisoner on the boat which had carried her and her father from France to England. "He was very good and kind to my father and to me," she said.

"Was he traveling alone on the ship?"

"No, he was with two French gentlemen."

"Now, Miss Manette, did you see him show them any papers, or anything that looked like a list?"

"No, I didn't see anything like that."

Questions, questions, questions! The trial went on, and finally a small, red-haired man spoke. He told the judge that he had seen Mr. Darnay at a hotel in a town where there were many soldiers and ships. Then one of the lawyers, a man called Sydney Carton, wrote some words on a piece of paper and gave it to Mr. Stryver, the lawyer who was speaking for Mr. Darnay.

"Are you quite sure that the prisoner is the man you saw?" Mr. Stryver asked the red-haired man.

"Quite sure," said the man.

"Have you ever seen anyone like the prisoner?" asked Mr. Stryver.

"I'd always be able to recognize him." The red-haired man was very confident.

"Then I must ask you to look at the gentleman over there," said Mr. Stryver, pointing to Sydney Carton. "Don't you think that he is very similar to the prisoner?"

Everyone in the court could see that Sydney Carton and Charles Darnay were indeed very similar.

"Well then," said Mr. Stryver, "it is so easy to find a man like the prisoner that we can even find one in this room. So how can you be so sure that it was the prisoner you saw in that hotel?"

And the red-haired man said not another word.

The lawyers talked and argued, and when at last the trial came to an end, Jerry Cruncher had fallen asleep.

But Mr. Lorry woke him up and gave him a piece of paper. "NOT GUILTY" were the words written on it, and Jerry hurried back to Tellson's Bank with the message.

"*I must ask you to look at the gentleman over there.*"

Sydney Carton seemed to be a man who did not care about anyone or anything. He was Mr. Stryver's assistant. In fact, he did most of the real work for Mr. Stryver. Stryver was good at speaking at a trial, but he was not good at discovering important facts and details, especially when these details were hidden in a lot of papers. Every night Carton studied the many papers that lawyers have to read, and he wrote down the questions which Stryver should ask at the next day's trial. And every day Stryver asked these questions, and people thought how clever he was.

Outside the Old Bailey Mr. Darnay, now a free man, met his friends: Dr. Manette and his daughter Lucie, Mr. Jarvis Lorry, Mr. Stryver, and Mr. Carton.

Dr. Manette no longer looked like the man in the room above Defarge's wine shop five years ago. His hair was white, but his eyes were bright and he stood straight and strong. Sometimes his face became dark and sad when he remembered the years in the Bastille prison; at these times only his daughter Lucie, whom he loved very much, could help him.

As they stood there talking, a strange expression came over Dr. Manette's face. He was staring at Charles Darnay, but he did not seem to see him. For a few moments there was dislike, even fear in his eyes. "My father," said Lucie softly, putting her hand on his arm, "shall we go home now?"

"Yes," he answered slowly.

Soon they drove off in a coach, and then Mr. Stryver and Mr. Lorry walked away, leaving Mr. Darnay and Mr. Carton alone.

"It must be strange for you," said Carton, "to be a free man again, and to be standing here, talking to a man who looks just like you. Let us go out and eat together."

After they had eaten, Carton said softly, "How sad and worried Miss Manette was for you today! She's a very beautiful young woman, don't you think?" *why?*

Darnay did not reply to what Carton had said, but he thanked him for his help at the trial.

"I don't want your thanks," replied Carton. "I have done nothing. And I don't think I like you." *Why?*

"Well," said Darnay, "you have no reason to like me. But I hope that you will allow me to pay the bill for both of us."

"Of course. And as you are paying for me, I'll have another bottle of wine." *rude*

After Darnay had left, Carton drank some more wine and looked at himself in the mirror. He was angry because Darnay looked so much like him, but was so different. Carton knew that he was a clever lawyer, and that he was a good and honest man, but he had never been successful for himself. He drank too much, and his life was unhappy and friendless. His cleverness and his hard work in the law only made others, like Mr. Stryver, successful and rich. He remembered Lucie Manette's worried face when she watched Darnay in court.

"If I changed places with Darnay," he whispered to himself, "would those blue eyes of Miss Manette look at me, in the same way? No, no, it's too late now."

He drank another bottle of wine and fell asleep.

In a quiet street not far away was the house where Dr. Manette and Lucie lived. They had one servant, Miss Pross, who had taken care of Lucie since she was a child. Miss Pross had red hair and a quick, sharp voice, and seemed at first sight a very alarming person. But everybody knew that she was in fact a warm-hearted and unselfish friend, who would do anything to guard her darling Lucie from trouble or danger.

Dr. Manette was now well enough to work as a doctor, and he, Lucie, and Miss Pross led a quiet, comfortable life. Mr.

*Miss Pross seemed at first sight a very alarming person.*

Lorry, who had become a close family friend, came regularly to the house, and in the months after the trial, Mr. Darnay and Mr. Carton were also frequent visitors. This did not please Miss Pross at all, who always looked very cross when they came.

"Nobody is good enough for my darling Lucie," she told Mr. Lorry one day, "and I don't like all these hundreds of visitors."

Mr. Lorry had a very high opinion of Miss Pross, but he wasn't brave enough to argue that two visitors were not "hundreds." Nobody argued with Miss Pross if they could avoid it.

# 4

## The Marquis of Evrémonde

The Marquis of Evrémonde was a disappointed man. He had waited for hours at the palace of the King of France, but the King had not spoken to him. Angrily, the Marquis got into his coach and told the driver to take him home. Very soon the coach was driving fast out of Paris, and the people in the narrow streets had to run to get out of the way if they could. At the corner of a street in Saint Antoine, one of the coach wheels hit something, and the people in the street screamed loudly. The horses were frightened and stopped.

"What has gone wrong?" asked the Marquis calmly, looking out of the window of the coach. A tall man had picked something up from under the feet of the horses and was crying loudly over it.

"Why is that man making that terrible noise?" asked the Marquis impatiently.

"I'm sorry, Monsieur the Marquis. It is his child," said one of the people.

"Dead! Killed!" screamed the man.

The people in the street came close to the coach and looked at the Marquis with stony, silent faces. The Marquis looked back at them in bored dislike. To him, they were no more than animals.

"I can't understand," he said coldly, "why you people cannot take care of yourselves and your children. I hope my horses are

15

not hurt." And he threw a gold coin to his driver. "Give this to that man!"

"Dead!" shouted the father of the child again.

Another man came forward. "Be brave, Gaspard. Your child has died quickly, and without pain. It is better to die like that than to go on living in these terrible times."

"You are a sensible man," said the Marquis from his coach. "What is your name?"

"They call me Defarge."

"This is for you," said the Marquis, and he threw Defarge another gold coin. "Drive on," he called to his driver.

Just as the coach was leaving, a coin was thrown back in through the window. The Marquis looked angrily at the corner where Defarge had been standing. Defarge had gone.

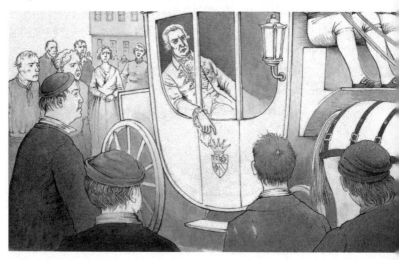

At the corner there now stood a large, dark-haired woman, knitting. She stared long and hard at the face of the Marquis, but he did not look at her and drove on.

Later that day, as the sun was going down, the same coach stopped in a village near the Marquis's castle. Several villagers, in poor thin clothes, with thin hungry faces, were standing in the village square. The Marquis looked at their faces and then pointed to one of them.

"Bring that man to me," he said to his driver.

The man came up to the coach, hat in hand, and the other villagers moved closer to listen.

"I passed you on the road just outside the village," said the Marquis. "You were looking at my coach in a very strange way. Why was that?"

*"Dead!" shouted the father of the child.*

"Monsieur, I was looking at the man," came the reply.

"What man?" asked the Marquis angrily.

"The man who was holding on under your coach," said the poor man, trembling with fear.

"What was he like?"

"Oh, Monsieur, he was white from head to foot. All covered with dust. Just like a ghost."

"Where is he now? What happened to him?"

"Oh, he ran away down the hill outside the village."

The Marquis turned to speak to another man. This was Monsieur Gabelle, the Marquis's official in the village.

"Gabelle," the Marquis said, "watch out for this man. If he comes here, put him in prison."

When the Marquis arrived at his castle, he asked if his nephew, Monsieur Charles, had arrived from England.

"Not yet, sir," replied the servant, but as the Marquis was eating his dinner, he heard the sound of a coach outside. Soon his nephew entered the room. In England he was known as Charles Darnay.

"You've been away for a long time," said the Marquis, with his cold, polite smile.

"I've had many problems in England. Perhaps because of you," Darnay said to his uncle. "I was in great danger."

"No, no, I had nothing to do with your problems," replied the Marquis coldly. "Unfortunately, our family no longer has the power that it once had."

"If it still had that power, one word from you would

doubtless send me to prison," said Darnay.

"Possibly. For the good of our family."

"The name of our family is hated everywhere in France. We are hard, cruel landowners. Our miserable people own nothing. They work for us night and day, but they don't even have enough food for themselves and their children. If this land became mine, I would give it away, and go and live somewhere else."

"You seem to be very fond of England, although you are not a rich man there," said the Marquis. "I believe you know another Frenchman who has found a safe home there. A doctor, I believe?"

"Yes."

"With a daughter?"

"Yes."

"Yes," said the Marquis with a secret smile on his face. "So, a new way of life begins. But you are tired. Goodnight, Charles. Sleep well. I will see you in the morning."

*"You seem to be very fond of England," said the Marquis.*

After his nephew had gone to bed, the Marquis went to his room. The castle was surrounded with darkness. In the villages nearby the hungry people dreamed of a better life, with enough good food to eat and time to rest from their work.

Early in the morning the dreamers awoke and started their day's hard work. The people in the castle did not get up until later, but when they did, why did the great bell start ringing? Why did people run out of the castle to the village as fast as they could?

*Why did people run out of the castle to the village*
*as fast as they could?*

The answer lay in the bed of the Marquis. He lay there, like stone, with a knife pushed into his heart. On his chest lay a piece of paper with the words:

*"Drive him fast to his grave. This is from JACQUES."*

# 5

## Two Men Speak of Love

Twelve months after the death of the Marquis in France, Charles Darnay had become a successful teacher of French in London. He had known, when he came to London, that he would have to work hard to earn his living, and he was successful. He was also in love. He had loved Lucie Manette from the time when his life was in danger in the Old Bailey. He had never heard a sound so sweet as her gentle voice; he had never seen a face so beautiful as hers. But he had never spoken to her about his love. The death of his uncle in France had become, over the twelve months, like a dream to him, but he had said nothing to Lucie of his feelings, nor of what had happened. He had good reason for this.

But one day in the summer he came to Dr. Manette's home in London. He knew that Lucie was out with Miss Pross, and he had decided to speak to her father. Dr. Manette was now strong in body and mind, and sad memories of his long years in prison did not come back to him often. When Darnay arrived, the Doctor welcomed him warmly.

"Dr. Manette," said Darnay, "I know that Lucie is out. But I have come here today to speak to you."

There was a silence. "Do you want to speak to me about Lucie?" asked the Doctor, slowly.

"Yes. Dear Dr. Manette, I love your daughter dearly. If there was ever love in the world, I love Lucie."

"I believe you," said Dr. Manette sadly. "It's very hard for me to speak of her at any time, but I believe you, Charles Darnay. Have you spoken to Lucie about your love?"

"No, never. I know how much your daughter means to you, Dr. Manette. Her love for you, and your love for her, these are the greatest things in your life, and in hers. I love Lucie. With all my heart I love her. But I do not want to come between you and her. The two of you will never be separated because of me."

For a moment Dr. Manette turned his head away, and his eyes were full of fear and pain. Then he looked back at Darnay and tried to smile.

"You have spoken very honestly, Charles," he said. "Have you any reason to believe that Lucie loves you?"

"None!"

"Then what do you want from me?"

"A promise. A promise that if Lucie ever tells you that she loves me, you will not speak against me and will tell her what I have said. I know that she would never accept me if she believed that it would make you unhappy."

"I can promise you more than that, Charles. If Lucie ever tells me that she loves you, I shall give her to you."

"Thank you, Dr. Manette," said Darnay, gratefully. "There is one thing more. My name in England is not my real name. I want to tell you what my real name is and why I am in England."

"Stop!" said the Doctor. He had even put his hands over his ears. "I don't want to know. Tell me when I ask you. If Lucie agrees to marry you, you shall tell me on the morning of your marriage."

It was dark when Darnay left Dr. Manette, and it was some time later when Lucie and Miss Pross came home.

"Father," Lucie called, "where are you?" She heard no answer, but there were strange sounds coming from her father's bedroom. Frightened, she ran upstairs and found her father, pale and silent, busy at his old prison work of making shoes. The shadow of the Bastille had fallen on him again. She took his arm and spoke gently to him, and together they walked up and down for a long time until at last Dr. Manette went quietly to bed.

Although Mr. Carton visited Dr. Manette's house quite often, he usually said very little when he was there. One day in August he arrived when Dr. Manette was out, and he was received by Lucie. She had always been a little shy with him, but on that day she noticed something different in his face.

"Aren't you well, Mr. Carton?" she asked.

"No, probably not, Miss Manette, but my way of life is not good for my health."

"That seems sad," said Lucie gently. "Why do you not change your way of life?"

"It's too late for that. I shall never be better than I am. But, Miss Manette, there is something that I want to say to you, but I find it very difficult. Will you listen to me?"

"If it will help you, Mr. Carton, I will be happy to listen to you," said Lucie, but she was pale and trembling.

23

"Miss Manette, I know that you could never have feelings of love for me, a man who has spent his life so badly."

"Even without my love, Mr. Carton, can I not save you? Can I not help you?"

"No, Miss Manette," said Carton. "Even if it was possible for you to love me, it is too late for me. I would only make you sad and destroy your life. But it has been a last dream of my heart. To see you and your father together, to see the home that you have made for him—this has brought back old and happier memories for me."

"Can I do nothing to help you?" asked Lucie sadly.

"Only this, Miss Manette. Let me remember that I spoke to you of the feelings of my heart, and that you were kind and gentle towards me."

*"It has been a last dream of my heart."*

"Oh, Mr. Carton. Try again to change."

"No, Miss Manette, it is too late. My bad habits will never change now. But tell me that you will never speak of what I have said today, not to anyone, not even to the person dearest to you."

"Mr. Carton," said Lucie. "This is your secret. No one will ever know of it from me."

"Thank you, Miss Manette. I shall never speak of this again. But in the hour of my death, it will be a happy memory for me that my last words of love were to you."

Lucie had never heard Mr. Carton speak like this before. Tears came to her eyes as she thought of his hopeless, miserable life.

"Don't cry," said Sydney Carton. "I am not worth your love. But you should know that for you, or for anyone close to you, I would do anything. Please remember always that there is a man who would give his life to keep someone you love alive and close to you. Goodbye, Miss Manette."

On the day of Lucie's marriage to Charles Darnay, Mr. Lorry and Miss Pross stood with Lucie outside the door of Dr. Manette's room. Inside, the Doctor and Mr. Darnay had been talking together for a long time.

Soon it would be time to leave for the church. Lucie looked very beautiful, and Mr. Lorry watched her proudly. He talked about the day, so long ago, when he had brought Lucie, as a baby in his arms, from France to England. Miss Pross, too, had her memories and thought fondly of her brother Solomon. He had stolen money from her many years ago, and she had never seen him since then, but she still loved him.

The door of the Doctor's room opened, and he came out with Charles Darnay. The Doctor's face was white, but he was calm. He took his daughter's arm, and they went out to the waiting coach. The others followed in a second coach and soon, in a nearby church, Lucie Manette and Charles Darnay were married.

After the marriage Lucie and Charles came back to the house for breakfast, and then Lucie had to say goodbye to her father for two weeks. This would be the first time they had not been together since his return from Paris.

When Lucie and Charles had left, Mr. Lorry noticed a change in the Doctor. A little sadness was natural, but there was a lost, frightened look in the Doctor's eyes, which worried Mr. Lorry very much. When he left to go to Tellson's Bank, he whispered to Miss Pross that he would return as quickly as he could.

Two hours later he hurried back to the house, and Miss Pross met him at the door.

"Oh, what shall we do, Mr. Lorry?" she cried. "He doesn't know me and is making shoes again!"

Mr. Lorry went up to the Doctor's room. "Dr. Manette, my dear friend. Look at me. Don't you remember me?"

But Dr. Manette said nothing and worked on in silence. Once again, he was a prisoner in the Bastille, without friends or family, without even a name of his own.

For nine days and nine nights the shoemaker worked on, leaving his table only to sleep, eat, or walk up and down his room. Mr. Lorry sat with him night and day, talking gently to him from time to time, trying to bring his friend's mind back to the present.

*For nine days and nine nights the shoemaker worked on.*

Then at last, on the tenth morning, the shoemaking work was put away, and Dr. Alexandre Manette, pale but calm, was his old self again. Lucie was never told, and in the quiet and happy years that followed her marriage, Dr. Manette remained strong in mind and body.

# 6

## Stormy Years in France

In Monsieur Defarge's wine shop in Saint Antoine customers came and went all the time. They came to drink the thin, rough wine, but more often they came to listen, to talk, and to wait for news.

One day there were more customers than usual. Defarge had been away for three days, and when he returned that morning, he brought a stranger with him, a man who repaired roads.

"Madame," Defarge said to his wife, "this man, who is called Jacques, has walked a long way with me." One customer got up and went out. "This mender of roads," continued Defarge, "who is called Jacques, is a good man. Give him something to drink." A second man got up and went out. The man who repaired roads sat down and drank. A third man got up and went out.

"Have you finished, my friend?" said Defarge. "Then come and see the room I promised you."

They went upstairs, to the room where Dr. Manette had sat making shoes. The three men who had left the wine shop were waiting. Defarge spoke to them.

"No names. You are Jacques One, Jacques Two, and Jacques Three. I am Jacques Four. This is Jacques Five. He brings us news of our poor friend Gaspard, whose child was killed by the Marquis's coach a year ago."

"I first saw Gaspard," said Jacques Five, "holding on under the Marquis's coach as it drove into our village. He ran away, but that night the Marquis was murdered. Gaspard disappeared and was only caught a few weeks ago. The soldiers brought him into the village and hanged him. And they have left his body hanging in the village square, where the women go to fetch water, and our children play."

*"And they have left his body hanging in the village square."*

When Jacques Five had left them, Jacques One said to his friends, "What do you say? Shall we put their names on the list?"

"Yes, all of them. The castle and all of the family of Evrémonde."

"Is the list safe?" asked Jacques Two.

"Yes, my friend," said Defarge. "My wife remembers

everything. But more than that, every name is carefully knitted into her work. Nothing can be forgotten."

A few days later Defarge reported to his wife some news from his friend "Jacques" in the police.

"A new spy has been sent to Saint Antoine. His name is Barsad, John Barsad. He's English."

"What does he look like? Do we know?"

"He's about forty years old, quite tall, black hair, thin face," said Defarge.

"Good," said his wife. "I'll put him on the list tomorrow. But you seem tired tonight. And sad."

"Well," said Defarge, "it is a long time."

"It takes time to prepare for change. The crimes against the people of France cannot be revenged in a day."

"But we may not live to see the end."

"Even if that happens," replied Madame Defarge, "we shall help it to come. But I believe that we shall see the day of our revenge against these hated noblemen."

The next day a stranger came into the wine shop. At once, Madame Defarge picked up a rose from the table and put it in her hair. As soon as they saw this, the customers stopped talking and, one by one, without hurrying, left the wine shop.

"Good day, Madame," said the stranger.

"Good day, Monsieur," said Madame Defarge, but to herself she said, "About forty years old, tall, black hair, thin face. Yes, I know who you are, Mr. John Barsad."

"Is business good?" asked the stranger.

"Business is bad. The people are so poor." Madame Defarge

looked over to the door. "Ah, here is my husband."

"Good day, Jacques," said the spy.

"You're wrong," said Defarge, staring at him. "That's not my name. I am Ernest Defarge."

"It's all the same," said the spy easily. "I remember something about you, Monsieur Defarge. You took care of Dr. Manette when he came out of the Bastille."

"That's true," said Defarge.

"Have you heard much from Dr. Manette and his daughter? They're in England now."

"No, not for a long time."

"She was married recently. Not to an Englishman, but to a Frenchman. It's quite interesting when you remember poor Gaspard. Miss Manette has married the nephew of the Marquis that Gaspard killed. Her new husband is really the new Marquis, but he prefers to live unknown in England. He's not a Marquis there, just Mr. Charles Darnay."

Monsieur Defarge was not happy at this news. When the spy had gone, he said to his wife, "Can it be true? If it is, I hope that Miss Manette keeps her husband away from France."

"Who knows what will happen?" replied Madame Defarge. "I only know that the name of Evrémonde is in my list, and for good reason." She went on calmly knitting, adding name after name to her list of the enemies of the people.

Time passed, and Madame Defarge still knitted. The women of Saint Antoine also knitted, and the thin hungry faces of Jacques and his brothers became darker and angrier. The noise of the coming storm in Paris was growing louder.

It began one summer day in the streets of Saint Antoine, around Defarge's wine shop, with a great crowd of people. A crowd who carried guns, knives, sticks, even stones—anything that could be a weapon. An angry crowd who shouted and screamed, who were ready to fight and to die in battle.

"Friends and citizens!" shouted Defarge. "We are ready! To the Bastille!" The crowd began to move, like the waves of the sea.

"Follow me, women!" cried Madame Defarge. A long sharp knife shone brightly in her hand. "We can kill as well as any man!"

The living sea of angry people ran through Saint Antoine to the Bastille, and soon the hated prison was ringing with the noise of battle. Fire and smoke climbed up the high stone walls and the thunder of the guns echoed through the city.

Four terrible and violent hours. Then a white flag appeared above the walls and the gates were opened. The Bastille had been taken by the people of Paris! Soon the crowds were inside the building itself, and shouting "Free the prisoners!" But Defarge put his strong hand on the shoulder of one of the soldiers.

"Show me the North Tower. Take me to One Hundred and Five, North Tower! Quickly!"

"Follow me," said the frightened man, and Defarge and Jacques Three went with him through the dark prison, past heavy closed doors, up stone stairs, until they came to a low door. It was a small room, with dark stone walls and only one very small window, too high for anyone to look out. Defarge

*Soon the hated prison was ringing with the noise of battle.*

looked carefully along the walls.

"There, look there, Jacques Three," he cried.

"A.M.!" whispered Jacques.

"A.M. Alexandre Manette," said Defarge softly. "Let us go now." But before they left, they searched the room and the furniture very carefully, looking for small hiding-places.

Then they returned to the crowds below. The Bastille and its officers were now in the hands of the people, and the people wanted revenge, and blood.

"At last, it has begun, my dear," said Defarge to his wife. It was the fourteenth of July, 1789.

In the village where the Marquis had lived and where Gaspard had died, life was hard. Everything was old and tired and broken down—the people, the land, the houses, the animals. In the past everything and everybody had had to work for the Marquis, and he had given nothing in return.

But now, strangers were traveling about the country, strangers who were poor, like the people, but who talked about new ideas—ideas which had started in Paris and were now running like fire across the country.

The road-mender who had brought the news of Gaspard to Paris still worked repairing the roads. One day a stranger came to him as he worked on the road outside the village.

"Jacques," said the stranger. He shook the road-mender's hand, and turned to look at the Marquis's castle on the hill. "It's tonight, Jacques," he went on quietly. "The others will meet me here."

It was very dark that night and the wind was strong. No one saw the four men who came quietly to the castle and said nothing. But soon the castle itself could be seen in the dark sky. The windows became bright; smoke and yellow flames climbed into the sky. Monsieur Gabelle called loudly for help, but the people in the village watched and did nothing to save the castle where the Marquis had lived.

# 7

## A Call for Help

The troubles in France continued. The citizens of France had fought to win power, and now they used it. Castles were burned, laws were changed, and the rich and powerful nobles died—their heads cut off by that terrible new machine of death, the Guillotine. In Paris the King was put in prison, and in 1792 the people of France sent him to the Guillotine as well. The French Revolution was now three years old, but there were more years of terror to come.

Not all the rich nobles had died. Some had escaped to England; some had even sent or brought their money to London before the Revolution began. And Tellson's Bank, which the French emigrants used, had become a meeting-place where they could hear and talk about the latest news from France.

One wet August day Mr. Lorry sat at his desk in the bank, talking to Charles Darnay. The years since Charles's marriage had seen the arrival of a daughter, little Lucie, who was now nine years old. Dr. Manette had continued in good health, and at the center of that warm family circle was always Lucie—a loving daughter, wife, mother, and a kind-hearted friend. Even Sydney Carton, though his old, bad ways were unchanged, was a family friend—and very much a favorite with little Lucie.

But at this moment Charles Darnay was trying very hard to persuade his old friend Mr. Lorry not to go to France. "It's too dangerous. The weather is not good, the roads are bad, and think of your age," he said.

"My dear Charles," said the banker. "You think that, at nearly eighty years of age, I'm too old. But that's exactly why *I* must go. I have the experience, I know the business. My work is to find and hide papers that might be dangerous to our customers. And anyway, Jerry Cruncher goes with me. He'll take good care of my old bones."

"I wish I could go," said Charles restlessly. "I feel sorry for the people in France, and perhaps I could help them. Only last night, when I was talking to Lucie—"

"Talking to Lucie," repeated Mr. Lorry. "You talk about your lovely wife at the same time as you talk about going to France. You must not go. Your life is here, with your family."

"Well, I'm not going to France. But you are, and I'm worried about you."

Just at that moment a bank clerk put an old, unopened

letter on Mr. Lorry's desk, and Darnay happened to see the name on it: The Marquis of Evrémonde, at Tellson's Bank, London. Since his uncle's death, this was Darnay's real name. On the morning of his wedding to Lucie he had told Dr. Manette, but the Doctor had made him promise to keep his name secret. Not even Lucie or Mr. Lorry knew.

"We can't find this Marquis," said the clerk.

"I know where to find him," said Darnay. "Shall I take the letter?"

"That would be very kind," said Mr. Lorry.

*"I know where to find him," said Darnay.*

As soon as he had left the bank, Darnay opened the letter. It was from Monsieur Gabelle, who had been arrested and taken to Paris.

*Monsieur, once the Marquis*
*I am in prison, and I may lose my life, because I worked for*
*a landowner who has left France. You told me to work for*
*the people and not against them, and I have done this. But*
*no one believes me. They say only that I worked for an*
*emigrant, and where is that emigrant? Oh Monsieur, please*
*help me, I beg you!*

This cry for help made Darnay very unhappy. After the death of the Marquis, he had told Gabelle to do his best for the people. But now Gabelle was in prison, just because he was employed by a nobleman. It was clear to Darnay that he must go to Paris. He did not think that he would be in danger, as he had done everything he could to help the people of his village. He hoped that he would be able to save his old servant.

That night Charles Darnay sat up late, writing two letters. One was to his wife, Lucie; the other was to her father, Dr. Manette. He told them where he had gone and why, and he promised that he would write to them from France. He had left secretly, he wrote, to save them from worrying.

The next day he went out, without saying anything to them of his plans. He kissed his wife and his daughter, and said that he would be back soon. And then he began his journey to Paris.

When he arrived in France, Darnay found that he could travel only very, very slowly towards Paris. The roads were bad and every town, every village had its citizens with guns who stopped all travelers, asked them questions, looked at their papers, made them wait or threw them in prison, turned them back or sent them on their way. And it was all done in the name of freedom—the new Freedom of France.

Darnay soon realized that he could not turn back until he had reached Paris and proved himself to be a good citizen, not an enemy of the people.

On his third night in France he was woken by an official and three other men with guns.

"Emigrant," said the official. "These three soldiers will take you to Paris, and you must pay them."

Darnay could only obey and at three o'clock in the morning he left with three soldiers to guard him. Even with them he was sometimes in danger; the people in the towns and villages all seemed to be very angry with emigrants, but finally they arrived safely at the gates of Paris. Darnay had to wait a long time while officials carefully read his papers, which explained the reasons for his journey. One official, seeing Gabelle's letter, looked up at Darnay in great surprise, but said nothing. Another official asked roughly,

"Are you Evrémonde?"

"Yes," replied Darnay.

"You will go to the prison of La Force!"

"But why?" asked Darnay. "Under what law?"

"We have new laws, Evrémonde," said the official sharply, "and emigrants have no rights. You will be held in secret. Take him away."

As Darnay left, the first official said quietly to him, "Are you the man who married the daughter of Dr. Manette?"

"Yes," replied Darnay in surprise.

"My name is Defarge and I have a wine shop in Saint Antoine. Perhaps you have heard of me."

"Yes. My wife came to your house to find her father."

"Why did you come back to France? It will be very bad for you."

Darnay was taken to the prison of La Force and put in a cold empty room with a locked door and bars across the windows. He thought of Dr. Manette and his many years alone, forgotten, in the Bastille.

"Now I, too, have been buried alive," he thought.

# 8

## In the Hands of the Citizens

Tellson's Bank in Paris was in a large building south of the river, close to the heart of the city. Mr. Lorry had arrived in Paris some days before Charles Darnay and was now living in some rooms above the bank. One evening, looking out of the window, he saw that a large grindstone had been brought into the square below. There was a wild, shouting crowd around it, busy sharpening their knives, swords, and axes, which were already red with blood. With shaking hands, Mr. Lorry closed the window.

*The crowd around the grindstone were busy sharpening
their knives, swords, and axes.*

He had decided to go downstairs and talk to the bank
guards, when suddenly the door of his room opened, and
Lucie and her father ran in.

"Lucie! Manette! What has happened? Why are you here?"
cried Mr. Lorry.

"Charles is in Paris," cried Lucie. "He came to help an old
family servant. But he's been taken to prison."

41

At that moment the shouts of the crowd outside grew louder.

"What is that noise?" asked the Doctor.

"Don't look out!" cried Mr. Lorry.

"My friend," said the Doctor. "I am safe in Paris. I was a prisoner in the Bastille. Everybody knows about me and how I suffered. Already people want to help me; they gave us news of Charles."

"Even so, don't look outside. Where is Charles?"

"In the prison of La Force."

"La Force! Dear Lucie, you can do nothing tonight. You must go to one of the rooms here and wait. I must talk with your father at once."

Lucie kissed him and left the room.

"Quick, Manette," said Mr. Lorry. "These people outside, with their bloody knives, are murdering the prisoners. If you are so well known, if you have this power, talk to them. Tell them who you are and go to La Force. Quick, before it is too late!"

Dr. Manette hurried outside. Mr. Lorry watched from the window as the Doctor talked to the crowd. He heard shouts of "Long live the Bastille prisoner! Help his friend in La Force!"

Mr. Lorry went to Lucie and found her with her daughter and Miss Pross. Together they waited all night for news, but none came.

In the morning Mr. Lorry found rooms for Lucie and her family in a quiet street near the bank. He left Jerry Cruncher with them as a guard and returned worriedly to Tellson's. At the end of the day a strong, serious man came to see him.

"My name is Defarge. I come from Dr. Manette; he gave me this." Defarge gave him a piece of paper.

The Doctor had written, *Charles is safe, but I cannot leave this place yet. Take Defarge to Lucie.*

"Come with me," said Mr. Lorry happily. They went downstairs and at the front door found Madame Defarge, knitting. Without a word, she joined them, and Mr. Lorry led them to Lucie's rooms.

There, Defarge gave Lucie a note from her husband.

*Dearest—be brave. I am well, and your father has some power here. You cannot answer this, but kiss our child for me.*

Only a short letter, but it meant so much to Lucie. Gratefully, she kissed the hands of Defarge and his wife. Madame Defarge said nothing; her hand was cold and heavy, and Lucie felt frightened of her.

*Gratefully, Lucie kissed the hands of Defarge and his wife.*

Miss Pross came in with little Lucie.

"Is that his child?" asked Madame Defarge, stopping her knitting to stare.

"Yes, Madame," said Mr. Lorry. "That is our poor prisoner's little daughter."

"It is enough, my husband," said Madame Defarge. "We can go now." Her voice was as cold as her hand.

"You will be good to my husband?" asked Lucie, afraid. "I beg you, as a wife and mother."

"We have known many wives and mothers," said Madame Defarge. "And we have seen many husbands and fathers put in prison for many years. What is one more, among so many?"

As the Defarges left, Lucie turned to Mr. Lorry. "I am more afraid of her than of any other person in Paris," she whispered. Mr. Lorry held her hands; he did not say anything, but he was also very worried.

The Doctor did not come back from La Force for several days. During that time eleven hundred prisoners were killed by the people. Inside the prison Dr. Manette had come before a Tribunal, which was a group of judges appointed by the people. These judges made their own laws and threw prisoners out into the streets to be murdered by the crowds. Dr. Manette told the Tribunal that he had been a prisoner in the Bastille for eighteen years and that his son-in-law was now a prisoner in La Force. The Tribunal had agreed to keep Charles Darnay safe from the murdering crowds, but they would not let him leave the prison.

Dr. Manette seemed to become stronger as he lived through

these terrible days, doing everything he could to save his daughter's husband. He was able to see Darnay regularly, but noblemen and emigrants were hated by the citizens of new France, and the Doctor could not set Darnay free. The Guillotine, that new machine of death, cut off the heads of many, many people—the powerful and the cruel, but also the beautiful, the innocent, and the good. Each day Lucie did not know if her husband would live or die. She lived every moment in great fear, but her father was sure that he could save his son-in-law.

One year and three months passed, and Darnay was still in prison. Dr. Manette now had an official job as doctor to three prisons and was able to visit Darnay regularly. He became

*Darnay was still in prison.*

45

more and more loved by the rough people of the Revolution. But the Guillotine continued to kill.

"Try not to worry," he told Lucie. "Nothing can happen to Charles. I know that I can save him." But Lucie could not see him or visit him; she could not even write to him.

On the day when Charles Darnay was at last called for his trial, Lucie and Dr. Manette hurried to Tellson's Bank to tell Mr. Lorry. As they arrived, a man got up and disappeared into another room. They did not see who it was, but in fact it was Sydney Carton, just arrived from London.

There were five judges in the Tribunal, and the trials were short and simple. The voices of truth, honesty, and calm reason were never heard at these trials, and most of the prisoners were sent to the Guillotine, which pleased the noisy crowds. Fifteen prisoners were called before Darnay that day, and in no more than an hour and a half, all of them had been condemned to death.

"Charles Evrémonde, who is called Darnay."

As Darnay walked in front of the judges, he tried to remember the careful advice that Dr. Manette had given him.

"Charles Evrémonde, you are an emigrant. All emigrants must die. That is the new law of France."

"Kill him!" shouted the people. "Cut off his head! He's an enemy of the people!"

The President of the judges asked Darnay, "Is it true that you lived many years in England?"

"Yes, that is true," replied Darnay.

"So you are an emigrant, surely."

"No, not in the meaning of the law," replied Darnay. "I earn my own living in England. I have never wanted or used the name of Marquis, and I did not want to live by the work of the poor people of France. So I went to live and work in England, long before the Revolution."

"And did you marry in England?"

"Yes, I married a Frenchwoman. The daughter of Dr. Manette, a prisoner of the Bastille and a well-known friend of all good citizens!"

These words had a happy effect on the crowd. Those who had shouted for his death now shouted for his life. Then Monsieur Gabelle and Dr. Manette spoke for Charles Darnay. The Doctor spoke well and clearly, and he was very popular with the crowd. When he had finished, the judges decided that the prisoner should be set free, and the crowd shouted their agreement loudly. Soon they were carrying Darnay in a chair through the streets of Paris to Dr. Manette's house. Lucie was waiting there, and when she ran out and fell into the arms of her husband, the men and women in the crowd kissed one another and danced for happiness. Darnay and Lucie were together again, safe and happy.

"I told you that I would save him," said Lucie's father proudly. "Well, I have saved him, and you must not worry now."

But Lucie was still worried. So many innocent men and women had died, for no reason, and every day brought more deaths. A shadow of fear and hate lay over France, and no one knew what dangers the next day would bring.

\* \* \*

It was not possible to leave Paris at once, as Charles did not have the necessary papers. They must live quietly and hope to leave as soon as they could.

But that night, when Dr. Manette, Charles, and Lucie were sitting together, they heard a loud knock at the door.

"What can this be?" said Lucie, trembling. "Hide Charles! Save him!"

"My child," said the Doctor, "I *have* saved him. He is a free man!"

But when he opened the door, four rough men pushed their way into the room.

"The Citizen Evrémonde, where is he? He is again the prisoner of the people."

*"The Citizen Evrémonde is again the prisoner of the people."*

"I am here," said Darnay. "But why am I again a prisoner?"

"You are accused by citizens of Saint Antoine."

Dr. Manette had said nothing. He seemed to be made of stone, but suddenly he spoke.

"Will you tell me who has accused my son-in-law?"

"I shouldn't tell you this," said one of the men, "but Citizen Evrémonde, called Darnay, is accused by Monsieur and Madame Defarge, and by one other person."

"What other?"

"You will hear that tomorrow," replied the man.

# 9

## The Spy

While this was happening, Miss Pross was out shopping for the family. Jerry Cruncher was with her, and they had just gone into a wine shop when Miss Pross suddenly stopped, looked at one of the customers, and cried out in a loud voice,

"Oh Solomon, dear Solomon! I've found you at last, dear brother! But whatever are you doing here in Paris?"

"Don't call me Solomon. You'll get me killed. Pay for your wine, and come outside," said the man in a low, frightened voice.

They went outside. "You mustn't recognize me here," said the man. "It's not safe. Go your way, and let me go mine."

Miss Pross began to cry at these unbrotherly words, and

Jerry Cruncher stepped forward to stare in the man's face.

"Wait a minute," said Jerry. "Is your name John Solomon, or Solomon John? Your sister calls you Solomon. I know that your name's John; I remember that. But your other name wasn't Pross at that Old Bailey trial. What was your name then?"

"*Barsad*!" said another voice.

"Yes, Barsad, that's it," cried Jerry. He turned around and saw Sydney Carton standing behind him.

"Don't be alarmed, my dear Miss Pross," said Carton, smiling at her. "But I'm afraid I have to tell you that your brother is a spy, a spy for the French prisons."

Solomon Pross, also Barsad, went pale. "That's not true!"

"I saw you come out of the Conciergerie today. I followed

*"I have to tell you that your brother is a spy," said Carton.*

50

you," said Carton, "and I found out what you do. And I've decided that you may be able to help me. Come with me to the office of Mr. Lorry."

After a short argument, which Carton won, Barsad followed him to Mr. Lorry's office.

"I bring bad news," Carton said to Mr. Lorry. "Darnay has been arrested again."

"But I was with him only two hours ago," cried Mr. Lorry. "He was safe and free!"

"Even so, he has been arrested and taken to the Conciergerie. And I'm not sure that Dr. Manette's good name can save him this time. So we must have Mr. Barsad's help."

"I will not help you," said Solomon Pross, called John Barsad.

"Oh, I think you will," said Sydney Carton, "when you hear what I could say about you. Let's think. Mr. Barsad is a spy, and a prison guard, but he used to be a spy in England. Is he still paid by the English?"

"No one will listen to you," said Barsad.

"But I can say more, Mr. Barsad," replied Carton.

Barsad had more problems than Carton knew. He could not return to England because he was wanted by the police there. And in France, before he became a prison guard for the citizens' revolution, he had been a spy for the King's officers. He knew that Madame Defarge, that terrible woman, had knitted his name into her list of enemies of the people. Most of those on her list had already been killed by the Guillotine, and Barsad did not want to be next.

"You seem worried, Mr. Barsad," said Carton calmly.

The spy turned to Mr. Lorry. "Miss Pross is my sister, sir. Would you send her brother to his death, sir?"

"The best thing for your sister, Mr. Barsad," said Carton smoothly, "is not to have a brother like you. I think I will inform the Tribunal that I suspect you of spying for England. You will be condemned at once, I am sure."

"All right," Barsad said slowly, "I'll help you. But don't ask me to do anything that will put my life in danger, because I won't do it."

"You're a guard at the Conciergerie prison, where Darnay is, aren't you?" said Carton. "Come, let us talk privately in the next room."

When Mr. Carton returned alone, Mr. Lorry asked what he had done.

"Not much," replied Carton, "but if it goes badly for Darnay tomorrow, I can visit him once. It's all I could do."

"But that will not save him," cried Mr. Lorry sadly.

"I never said it would."

Mr. Lorry was an old man now, with a life of hard work behind him. Tears filled his eyes as he realized he could do nothing to help Lucie and her father now.

Sydney Carton felt very sorry for Mr. Lorry. "You're a good friend of Dr. Manette and his daughter, but don't tell them about me or this meeting. It can't help Lucie." He paused. "Will you go back to London soon?"

"Yes, my work for Tellson's Bank here is finished. I have the necessary papers to leave Paris. I was ready to go tomorrow."

"Then don't change your plans," said Carton, very seriously.

Later that night Sydney Carton visited a shop in a quiet corner of Paris. He wrote on a piece of paper the names of several powders and gave it to the shopkeeper.

"For you, citizen?" asked the shopkeeper.

"Yes, for me."

"You must be careful, citizen. Keep these things separate. You know what happens if you put them together."

"Perfectly," replied Carton.

He spent the rest of that night walking the streets of Paris. He watched the moon rise in the sky, he listened to the sounds of the River Seine flowing through the heart of the city, and he thought calmly about the past, and the future. He thought about all the deaths that the city had already seen ... and he thought about Lucie's gentle, loving face and her sad, sad eyes.

*Carton spent the rest of that night walking the streets of Paris.*

# 10

## The Secret Paper

When Charles Darnay was led before the Tribunal the next morning, Dr. Manette, Lucie and Mr. Lorry were all there. The love in Lucie's eyes as she looked at her husband warmed Darnay's heart. It had the same effect on Sydney Carton, though no one saw him standing at the back of the room.

It was the same Tribunal who had let Darnay go free on the day before. But Revolution Laws were not as powerful as the anger of the people.

The President of the Tribunal asked, "Who has accused Charles Evrémonde again?"

"Three voices," he was told. "He is accused by Ernest Defarge, by Teresa Defarge, his wife, and by Alexandre Manette, Doctor."

There was a great noise in the room when Dr. Manette's name was heard. When the shouting stopped, Dr. Manette stood, pale and trembling.

"President, this cannot be true. You know that the man who is accused, Charles Darnay, is my daughter's husband. My daughter and those who are dear to her are far more important to me than my life. Where is the liar who says that I accuse my daughter's husband?"

"Citizen Manette," said the President, "be calm. Nothing can be more important to a good citizen than the freedom of France."

*"Where is the liar who says that I accuse
my daughter's husband?"*

Defarge came forward to answer questions. He told how he had been at the Bastille at the beginning of the Revolution, when that hated prison had been taken by the citizens.

"I knew that Dr. Manette had been kept in a room known as One Hundred and Five, North Tower. It was the only name he had when he came to me in 1775. I went to the room and, hidden in a hole, I found a written paper. It is in Dr. Manette's writing."

"Read it to us," said the President, and the crowd fell silent and listened.

I, Alexandre Manette, write this in the Bastille in 1767. I have been here for ten long years, and I write this in my secret moments, when I can.

One evening in December, 1757, I was walking by the River Seine when a coach stopped beside me. Two men got out, and one asked me if I was Dr. Manette. When I replied that I was, they asked me to go with them and made it clear that I could not refuse.

The coach left Paris and stopped at a lonely house. I could hear cries coming from a room upstairs. When I went in, I saw a young woman lying on a bed. She was young and very beautiful. She was also very ill. She kept crying out, "My husband, my father, and my brother!" Then she listened for a moment, and began once again, "My husband, my father, and my brother …"

I gave the girl something to make her calmer, but her feverish screams continued. Then I turned to question the two men. They were clearly brothers, and their clothes and voices suggested that they were noblemen. But they took care to prevent me from learning their name.

Before I could speak, the older brother said carelessly, "There is another patient." In a different room, they showed me a boy of about seventeen. There was a sword wound in his chest, and I could see at once that he was dying.

"How did this happen?" I asked.

"He's just a crazy young peasant. He came here shouting about revenge and made my brother fight him." The older brother's voice was cold and hard; he seemed to think the boy was less important than a horse or a dog.

The boy's eyes looked at me. "Have you seen her ... my sister?" It was hard for him to speak.

"I have seen her," I replied.

"These rich nobles are cruel to us, Doctor. They destroy our land, they take our food, and they steal our sisters. My sister loved a man in our village; he was sick, but she married him to take care of him. But my sister is beautiful, and that nobleman's brother saw her and wanted her. They made her husband work night and day without stopping, until he dropped dead where he stood. Then they took my sister away. When my father heard what had happened, the news was too much for his poor heart and he died suddenly. I took my younger sister to a place where she is safe and came here to find this man. He threw some money at me and tried to buy me like a dog, but I made him pull his sword and fight me to save his life."

The boy's life was going fast, but he cried, "Lift me, Doctor." He turned his face towards the older brother. "Marquis," he said loudly, "I call for you and your brother, and all your family, now and in the future, to pay for what you have done." Then he fell back, dead.

The young woman's fever continued, but I could not save her. She lived for several more days, and once the Marquis said to me, "How long these peasants take to die!"

When she was dead, the brothers warned me to keep silent. They offered me money, but I refused it and was taken back to my home.

The next day I decided to write to the King's officials. I knew that nobles who did unlawful things were usually not punished, and I expected that nothing would happen. But I did not realize the danger for myself. Just as I had finished writing my letter, a lady came to see me. She said she was the wife of the Marquis of Evrémonde, and she had discovered what her husband and his brother had done. She wanted to help the younger sister of the girl who had died and asked me where she could find her. Sadly, I did not know, and so could not tell her. But that was how I learned the brothers' name.

The wife of the Marquis was a good, kind woman, deeply unhappy in her marriage. She had brought her son with her, a boy about three years old. "If I cannot find this poor girl," she said, "I shall tell my son to continue the search after my death. You will remember that, little Charles, won't you?"

The child answered, "Yes!"

Later that day I sent my letter to the King's officials, and that night there was a knock at my door. My servant, a boy called Ernest Defarge, brought in a stranger, who asked me to come at once to visit a sick man in the next street.

As soon as I was outside the house, several men took hold of me violently. The Evrémonde brothers came out of the darkness, and the Marquis took my letter out of his pocket, showed it to me, and burned it. Not a word was spoken. Then I was brought here to this prison, my living grave.

I have been here for ten long years. I do not know if my dear wife is alive or dead; these brothers have sent me no news of my family. There is no goodness in their cruel hearts. I, Alexandre Manette, in my pain and sadness, I condemn them in the face of God.

When Defarge had finished reading, a terrible sound rose from the crowd, a long wild cry of anger and revenge. Death for the hated Marquis of Evrémonde, enemy of the people! The trial was over, and in less than twenty-four hours Charles Darnay would go to the Guillotine.

# II

## Madame Defarge's Revenge

Lucie held out her arms to her husband. "Let me kiss him, one last time."

Most of the citizens had gone out into the streets to shout how they hated the prisoners, but Barsad was still there.

"Let her kiss her husband," he said. "It's just for a minute."

Lucie went over to her husband, and he took her in his arms. Dr. Manette followed his daughter and fell on his knees before them, but Darnay pulled him to his feet, saying,

"No, no. Now we know how much you suffered, especially when you knew whose son I was. But you kept your feelings secret, because of your love for Lucie. We thank you, with all our hearts, for what you did. I tried so hard to do what my mother had wished, but I never found that poor girl. And how could that terrible story ever have a happy ending?"

He turned to his wife. "My dearest love, we shall meet again, in the place where there are no worries. God be with you both."

As Darnay was taken away, Lucie fell to the floor, unconscious. Sydney Carton came quickly forward to help Mr. Lorry and Dr. Manette. He carried Lucie to her coach, and she was taken home. Then he carried her into the house where her daughter and Miss Pross waited, tears falling from their eyes.

"Before I go," said Sydney Carton, "may I kiss her?" He touched Lucie's face lightly with his lips, whispered a few words, and went into the next room.

"You are still very popular with the citizens, Doctor. You must try again to talk to the judges."

"I'll do everything I can. Everything," Dr. Manette said.

Mr. Lorry went with Carton to the door.

"I have no hope," whispered Mr. Lorry sadly.

"Nor have I," replied Carton. "After today, no judge in Paris would even try to save him. The people would be too angry. I will return here later, to see if there is any news, but there is no real hope."

He left the house and began to walk quickly towards Saint Antoine. His face was calm and serious; he looked like a man who had decided to do something. "I must show myself to the people here," he thought. "They should know that there is a man like me in the city."

In Defarge's wine shop the only customer was Jacques Three, who had been on the Tribunal that had decided Darnay should die. When Carton sat down and asked for a glass of wine, Madame Defarge looked at him carelessly at first. Then much more carefully. She went back to her husband and Jacques Three, who were talking. "He is very much like Evrémonde," she said softly.

Defarge himself looked at Carton and said, "Yes, but only a little," and the three continued their conversation. Carton

*"He is very much like Evrémonde," said Madame Defarge softly.*

listened carefully, while pretending to read a newspaper.

"Madame is right," said Jacques Three. "Why should we stop at Evrémonde?"

"We must stop somewhere," said Defarge.

"Not until they are all dead, every one of that family," said his wife.

"You're right, but think how much the Doctor has suffered. Perhaps he has suffered enough."

"Listen," said Madame Defarge coldly. "Don't forget that *I* was that younger sister. And it was *my* family that suffered so much from the Evrémonde brothers. It was *my* sister who died, and *my* sister's husband, and *my* father; it was *my* brother who was killed. Tell others to stop; don't tell me!"

Carton paid for his wine and went out quickly on his way. He went back to Dr. Manette's house, where more bad news was waiting for him. The Doctor's mind had returned to the past once again. He did not recognize his friends and wanted only to find his old table and to make shoes.

"Listen to me carefully," Carton said to Mr. Lorry. "I believe that Lucie, her daughter, and perhaps even her father are in great danger. I heard Madame Defarge talking about them tonight. They must leave Paris tomorrow. They have the necessary papers, and so do you. Here are mine—take them and keep them safe with your own. You must leave by coach at two o'clock tomorrow. Keep a place for me in the coach, and don't leave without me. Promise that you will do exactly what I have said. Many lives will depend on it."

"I promise," said Mr. Lorry.

# 12

## A Change of Clothes

Charles Darnay passed his last night alone in the prison. He had no hope. He knew he must die, not for anything he had done wrong, but for the crimes of his father and his uncle. He sat down to write to his wife:

*I knew nothing about the time your father spent in prison until he told me. Even then I did not know that it was my family that had been so cruel to him. I told your father that my real name was Evrémonde, and he made me promise not to tell you. I am sure that he had forgotten the paper he had written, but what has happened now is not his fault. Take care of him and our child, and one day we shall all meet again in the happier world that comes after death.*

Darnay did not sleep peacefully that night, and in the morning he walked up and down his prison, waiting. He counted the hours—nine, gone for ever, ten, eleven, twelve gone for ever. At one o'clock he heard someone outside the door. The door opened and closed, and there stood Sydney Carton, holding a warning finger to his lips.

"Be quiet! I come from your wife. She begs you to do exactly what I say and to ask no questions. There is no time. Take off your boots, and put on mine."

"Carton, my dear friend," said Darnay, "it is impossible to escape from this place. You will only die with me."

"I'm not asking you to escape. Put on my shirt and my coat."

He did not allow Darnay time to argue or refuse. "Now sit down and write what I say," he said. "Quickly, my friend, quickly!"

"*If you remember,*" he said, and Darnay wrote, "*the words we spoke so long ago, you will understand this when you see it.*" As he said this, Carton took his hand from his pocket.

"What is that in your hand?" asked Darnay.

"Nothing. Have you written '*see it*'? Good, now go on writing," said Carton quietly. "*I am happy that I can prove them now. This is not a reason for sadness.*" Carton's hand was close to Darnay's face, and he gently pressed a cloth against Darnay's nose and mouth. A minute later Darnay lay unconscious on the ground. Carton quickly dressed himself in

*Carton's hand was close to Darnay's face.*

Darnay's clothes and pushed the note that Darnay had written inside Darnay's pocket. Then he went to the door and called softly, "Come in now."

The spy Barsad came in.

"Quick, help me," said Carton. "You must help me to the coach."

"You?" asked the spy.

"Him, man. I've changed places with him. You can say that it was too much for him, saying his last goodbye to his friend. That happens quite often, I believe."

"Yes, often," replied Barsad. "But do you promise to keep me out of danger and go on with this plan to the end? The number must be right. Fifty-two prisoners must die today."

"Have I not already promised to be true to the death? Hurry, man! Take him to Mr. Lorry, put him in the coach yourself, and tell Mr. Lorry to leave at once!"

Barsad called two men into the room and told them to lift the unconscious man and carry him out.

"The time is short, Evrémonde," said Barsad, in a warning voice.

"I know it well," replied Carton. "Be careful with my friend, and leave me."

The door closed, and Carton was left alone. He listened carefully, but there were only normal prison sounds. No shouts, and no alarm bells. He waited calmly.

Soon he heard the sound of doors opening. The door of his prison cell opened, and a man said, "Follow me, Evrémonde!" and Carton followed him into a large, dark room.

There were many people there, some standing, some sitting, some walking about, some crying. Most of them stood, silent, looking at the ground. A young woman came up to him; she was thin and pale.

"Citizen Evrémonde," she said. "I was with you in La Force."

"True," he said softly, "but I forget what you were accused of."

"I am innocent. What could a poor little thing like me do? I am not afraid to die, Citizen Evrémonde, but I have done nothing."

Her sad smile as she said this touched Carton's heart.

"They say that the Revolution will do so much good for the poor people," said the girl. "How can my death help the poor? If it is true, I am willing to die, but I do not know how that can be. I heard that you were set free, Citizen Evrémonde," she went on. "I hoped it was true."

"It was, but I was taken again and condemned."

"When we go from here, Citizen Evrémonde, will you let me hold your hand? I am not afraid, but I am little and weak, and it will help to make me brave." The young girl looked into his face, and he saw a sudden doubt come into her eyes, followed by surprise. He touched his lips with his finger.

"Are you dying for him?" she whispered.

"And his wife and child. Yes."

"Oh, will you let me hold your brave hand, stranger?"

"Yes, my poor sister, to the last."

# 13

## The Last Goodbyes

At that same hour in the early afternoon a coach going out of Paris drives up to the gates of the city.

"Who goes there? Show us your papers!" The guard looks at the papers. "Alexandre Manette, Doctor. Which is he?"

This is Dr. Manette; this helpless old man, whispering crazily to himself.

"The last few days of the Revolution have been too much for him," said the guard with a cruel laugh. "Lucie his daughter. The wife of Evrémonde. Which is she?"

This is she. With her child, little Lucie, beside her.

*"Show us your papers!"*

"Hah, your husband has another meeting today. Sydney Carton. Lawyer, English. Which is he?"

He is here, in the corner. He is not well.

"And Jarvis Lorry. Banker, English. Which is he?"

"I am he, and the last," says Jarvis Lorry.

"Here are your papers, Jarvis Lorry. You may go."

There are wildly beating hearts in the coach, and trembling hands; there is the heavy breathing of the unconscious traveler. But onwards the coach goes; the horses are fast, and there are no shouts behind them on the road.

Also that afternoon Madame Defarge was talking with her friends.

"My husband is a good citizen, but he is not strong enough. He feels sorry for the Doctor. I say that all the Evrémonde people must go to the Guillotine. The wife and the child must follow the husband."

"They're both fine heads for the Guillotine," said Jacques Three. "Their heads will be a pretty sight when they are shown to the people. Yes, they too, must die."

"But I'm afraid that my husband may warn them and let them escape," Madame Defarge went on, "and I must do something myself. After the death of Evrémonde at three this afternoon we'll go to the Tribunal and accuse them."

The others agreed willingly. "No one must escape. More heads must fall."

"Lucie Manette will be at home now, waiting for the moment of her husband's death," said Madame Defarge. "I will go to her. She will say things against the Revolution and condemn herself. Here, take my knitting, and keep my usual seat near the Guillotine."

"Don't be late," said her friend.

"To see the death of Evrémonde, I shall not be late," replied the cruel voice of Madame Defarge.

There were many women in Paris at that time who hated the nobles and wanted to see them die. But of all these women, Madame Defarge was the one most feared. All her life she had been filled with hate. It was nothing to her that an innocent man was going to die because of his father's and his uncle's crimes. She wanted more. Hidden in her clothes were a gun and a sharp knife, and with her usual confident step, she began to walk to Dr. Manette's house.

The house was not yet empty. Miss Pross and Jerry Cruncher were there, preparing to follow Mr. Lorry's coach. Mr. Lorry had decided that two coaches were better than one; with fewer passengers, each coach would travel faster. But Miss Pross was still worried. A second coach leaving from the house might suggest an escape.

"Mr. Cruncher," she said, "you must go and stop our coach coming here. Drive to the church instead, and I'll meet you there at three o'clock."

Jerry hurried away. It was twenty past two, and at once Miss Pross began to get herself ready to leave. She was washing her face when she suddenly looked up and saw a figure standing in the room.

Madame Defarge looked at her coldly. "The wife of

Evrémonde—where is she?"

Miss Pross quickly stood in front of the door to Lucie's room. "You're a cruel, dangerous woman, but you won't frighten me," she said, breathing hard.

Each woman spoke in her own language, and neither understood the other's words. But Madame Defarge knew that Miss Pross was a true friend of the Doctor's family, and Miss Pross knew that Madame Defarge was the family's enemy.

"I wish to see the wife of Evrémonde. Go and tell her. Do you hear me?" said Madame Defarge. She stared angrily at Miss Pross, but Miss Pross stared back just as angrily.

"I am desperate," said Miss Pross. "I know that the longer I can keep you here, the greater hope there is for my darling girl. If you fight me, I'll fight back!"

Madame Defarge stepped forward and called loudly, "Citizen Doctor! Wife of Evrémonde! Answer me!"

There was no answer and Madame Defarge quickly opened three of the doors and saw that the rooms were empty. One door was still closed.

"If they are not in that room, they are gone. But they can be followed and brought back." She went towards the door, but Miss Pross jumped forward and held her around the waist. Madame Defarge was used to the fighting in the streets and was strong, but love is stronger than hate and Miss Pross did not let go. Madame Defarge tried to pull out her knife.

"No," said Miss Pross, "it's under my arm. You shall not have it."

Madame Defarge put her hand to the front of her dress and

began to pull out the gun. Miss Pross looked down, saw what it was, and hit out at it wildly. There was a loud bang, and a cloud of smoke, and Miss Pross stood alone, trembling with terror.

All this in a second. As the smoke cleared, Miss Pross saw

*Miss Pross hit out at the gun wildly.*

the lifeless body of Madame Defarge on the ground. In horror, she opened her mouth to call for help, but then she thought of the dangers this would bring for her dear Lucie. With shaking hands, she got her hat and coat, locked the door of the room, and went downstairs. As she crossed the bridge on the way to the church, she dropped the key of the locked room in the river and hurried on to meet Jerry Cruncher.

\*   \*   \*

As the death-carts carry the condemned prisoners through the streets of Paris, crowds watch to see the faces of those who are to die. In the chairs around the Guillotine, the friends of Madame Defarge are waiting for her. "Teresa, Teresa Defarge! Who has seen her? She's never missed before!"

But the death-carts have arrived, and the Guillotine has already begun its work. Crash!—A head is held up, and the women who sit knitting count, "One."

The supposed Evrémonde helps the young girl down from the cart. He carefully places her with her back to the Guillotine, and she looks up gratefully into his face.

"Because of you, dear stranger, I am calm. I think you were sent to me by God," she whispers.

"Or perhaps He sent you to me," says Sydney Carton. "Keep

*"Keep your eyes on me, dear child, and*
*do not think of anything else."*

your eyes on me, dear child, and do not think of anything else."

"I do not mind while I hold your hand. I shall not mind when I let it go, if they are quick."

"They are quick. Fear not!"

She kisses his lips; he kisses hers. Now the Guillotine is waiting. The young girl goes next, before him. The women count, "Twenty-Two", and Carton walks forward.

Twenty-Three.

They said of him that it was the most peaceful face ever seen there. What passed through Sydney Carton's mind as he walked those last steps to his death? Perhaps he saw into the future …

"I see Barsad, Defarge, the judges, all dying under this terrible machine. I see a beautiful city being built in this terrible place. I see that new people will live here, in real freedom. I see the lives for whom I give my life, happy and peaceful in that England which I shall never see again. I see Lucie when she is old, crying for me on this day every year, and I know that she and her husband remember me until their deaths. I see their son, who has my name, now a man. I see him become a famous lawyer and make my name famous by his work. I hear him tell his son my story.

"It is a far, far better thing that I do, than I have ever done; it is a far, far better rest that I go to, than I have ever known."

✳

# GLOSSARY

**citizen**  someone who belongs to a country or city

**condemn**  to say at a law trial that someone must be punished

**emigrant**  someone who leaves his or her own country to live in another country

**grave**  a hole in the ground where a dead person is buried

**guillotine**  a machine with a big knife for cutting people's heads off

**guilty**  you are guilty if it is proved at a law trial that you have done something wrong

**hang**  to kill someone by holding them above the ground with a rope around their neck

**innocent**  you are innocent if you are accused of a crime but did not do it

**knit**  to use long sticks to make clothes from wool

**Marquis**  the title of a nobleman

**memory**  something that you remember

**nobleman**  someone belonging to an important, titled family

**pale**  with little color in the face

**peasant**  a poor farmer who owns or rents a small piece of land

**powerful**  strong or important enough to make other people do what you want

**revolution**  when people fight to change the way their country is controlled

**servant**  someone who is paid to work in another person's house

**suffer**  to feel pain, sadness, etc. in body or mind

**terror**  very great fear

**tribunal**  a group of people who are judges at some kinds of trial

# A Tale of Two Cities

## ACTIVITIES

## *Before Reading*

1 **Read the back cover and the story introduction on the first page of the book. Answer these questions.**

   1 What are the "Two Cities" of the title?

   2 Where was the prisoner kept?

   3 What is his daughter's name?

   4 Who killed the Marquis?

   5 What is the Guillotine?

2 **Can you guess what is going to happen in this story? Circle Y (yes) or N (no) for each sentence.**

   1 Lucie and her family will be killed. Y/N

   2 She will have secrets from her family. Y/N

   3 Lucie's father will be sent to prison again. Y/N

   4 He will make money from selling shoes. Y/N

   5 Revolution will change everybody's lives. Y/N

   6 Innocent people will die. Y/N

3 **Why do you think the French Revolution happened? Choose the best words to complete this passage.**

In France in the *19th/18th* century *poor/rich* noblemen owned *most/none* of the land, and the poor had *nothing/everything*. They had *easy/hard* lives, *had/did not have* enough to eat, and *loved/hated* the King and his noblemen.

# *While Reading*

**Read Chapters 1 to 3, and then answer these questions.**

*Who*

1 ... brought a message for Mr. Lorry on the Dover road? *Jerry*

2 ... had brought Lucie back to England as a small child? *Lorry*

3 ... owned the wine shop in Paris? *Monsieur Defarge*

4 ... sat in the wine shop, knitting and watching? *madame defarge*

5 ... thought his name was 105, North Tower? *Dr. menette*

6 ... was the prisoner at the Old Bailey trial? *Charles*

7 ... looked very like the prisoner at the trial? *Carton*

8 ... had taken care of Lucie since she was a child? *miss pross*

**Read Chapters 4 and 5. Choose the best question-word for these questions, and then answer them.**

*What / How / Who*

1 *Who* died under the wheels of the Marquis's coach? *a child*

2 *How* did Gaspard travel to the Marquis's castle? *coach*

3 *How* did Charles Darnay feel about his French family? *abused*

4 *What* happened to the Marquis? *dead*

5 *Who* was in love with Lucie Manette? *charles, sedner*

6 *What* did Sydney Carton ask Lucie to remember always? *there is a man who would give his life for her*

7 *What* did Darnay tell Dr. Manette on the morning of his marriage to Lucie? *told his real name.*

8 *What* effect did this news have on Dr. Manette?

**Read Chapters 6 and 7. Who said this, and who or what were they talking about?**

1  "They have left his body hanging in the village square."
2  "It takes time to prepare for change."
3  "It's all the same."
4  "Friends and citizens! We are ready!"
5  "He'll take good care of my old bones."
6  "I know where to find him."
7  "Now I, too, have been buried alive."

**Read Chapters 8 and 9. Are these sentences true (T) or false (F)? Rewrite the false sentences with the correct information.**

1  Dr. Manette was in danger in Paris.
2  Madame Defarge was very afraid of Lucie.
3  Darnay was in a Paris prison for more than a year.
4  Not many of the prisoners were sent to the Guillotine.
5  John Barsad's real name was Solomon Pross.
6  Barsad refused to help Sydney Carton in any way.
7  Mr. Lorry was planning to stay in Paris for some time.

**Read Chapters 10 and 11. Match these halves of sentences, and use the linking words to make a paragraph of nine sentences. (Use each word once.)**

*and / because / because / however / that / until / when / where / which / who*

1  Darnay appeared before the Tribunal a second time, _____
2  _____ Dr. Manette heard that *he* was one of the accusers,

3 But Defarge explained that he had found a paper written by Dr. Manette in the Bastille, _____

4 The paper told a story of the Evrémonde brothers, _____

5 The people were so angry to hear of these crimes _____

6 After the trial, Sydney Carton went to the Defarges' wine shop, _____

7 Madame Defarge did not want to stop the killing _____

8 Dr. Manette could do nothing to help Darnay _____

9 Carton, _____, had a plan, _____

10 had caused the deaths of four members of a family.

11 his mind had returned to the past.

12 he was accused by three citizens.

13 he kept to himself.

14 he heard Madame Defarge talking about her family.

15 he read it aloud to the Tribunal.

16 he spoke angrily to the Tribunal.

17 they said Darnay must go to the Guillotine the next day.

18 all the Evrémonde family were dead.

**Before you read Chapters 12 and 13, can you guess the answers to these questions? The titles of the chapters are:**

*A Change of Clothes*
*The Last Goodbyes*

1 Who is going to change clothes, and why?

2 Who will be in the coach leaving Paris tomorrow?

3 What will happen to Ernest and Teresa Defarge?

4 Who is going to say "their last goodbyes"?

## *After Reading*

1 **Can you remember who's who? Match the characters to their descriptions.**

| | |
|---|---|
| Lucie Manette | the killer of the Marquis |
| Jarvis Lorry | once a prisoner in the Bastille |
| Madame Defarge | a lawyer |
| Dr. Manette | Miss Pross's brother |
| Charles Darnay | the doctor's daughter |
| Sydney Carton | an old friend of the Manettes |
| John Barsad | a good knitter |
| Gaspard | the Marquis's nephew |

2 **Which characters spent most of their lives in Paris, and which in London? Check one box each time.**

| | PARIS | LONDON |
|---|---|---|
| Ernest Defarge | ☐ | ☐ |
| Jarvis Lorry | ☐ | ☐ |
| Sydney Carton | ☐ | ☐ |
| Lucie Manette | ☐ | ☐ |
| Dr. Manette | ☐ | ☐ |
| Jerry Cruncher | ☐ | ☐ |
| Gaspard | ☐ | ☐ |
| Mr. Stryver | ☐ | ☐ |
| the Marquis of Evrémonde | ☐ | ☐ |
| Gabelle | ☐ | ☐ |

3 **On the morning of his marriage, Charles Darnay talked to Dr. Manette. Put their conversation in the right order and put in the speakers' names. Darnay speaks first (number 5).**

1 _____ "Very well, then. Who are you?"

2 _____ "Dr. Manette, you look so pale! Does this name hold memories for you?"

3 _____ "Yes, I remember. But *must* you tell me?"

4 _____ "Are you sure, Dr. Manette? When I spoke the name, I thought you had seen a ghost."

5 _____ "Dr. Manette, we said I would tell you my real name on the morning of my marriage—you remember?"

6 _____ "Some things are best kept secret, that's all. But come, we must go—my daughter is waiting."

7 _____ "There are many ghosts in my past, Charles. But I am quite sure. The name means nothing to me."

8 _____ "My name is Evrémonde, and since my uncle died, I have been the Marquis of Evrémonde. But I am not proud of this name, and I will never use it."

9 _____ "No, no. No, not at all. I have never heard the name before."

10 _____ "Yes, I must. I cannot marry your daughter without telling you who I really am."

11 _____ "Yes, I promise. But why must it be a secret?"

12 _____ "Then may I tell Lucie, too?"

13 _____ "Evrémonde!"

14 _____ "No! Promise me, Charles, that you will never tell Lucie, or anyone else, that your name is Evrémonde."

4 **Writers like Dickens often repeated words, or used words with opposite meanings, in the same sentence, for effect. Match these parts of sentences from the story and complete them with the best words.**

  1 It was the best of times,

  2 It was the spring of hope,

  3 It was the season of light,

  4 It was a strange message,

  5 It is a far, far better thing that I do, than I have ever done;

  6 and a _____ answer.

  7 it is a _____ rest that I go to, than I have ever known.

  8 it was the _____ of times.

  9 it was the season of _____.

 10 it was the _____ of sadness.

5 **Now complete these sentences about the story in the same way, in your own words.**

  1 Sydney Carton and Charles Darnay looked very similar, but their characters . . .

  2 Life in France was easy for the rich, but it was . . .

  3 When the Marquis killed a child, the child's father . . .

  4 The Revolution killed those who were guilty; it also . . .

  5 Miss Pross was a friend of Dr. Manette's family, but Madame Defarge . . .

  6 Charles Darnay loved Lucie and lived, but Sydney Carton . . .

6 Before Charles Darnay went to France to help Gabelle, he wrote a letter to Lucie (see page 38). Find the best word for each gap and complete his letter.

My dearest wife,

    I am _____ for France very soon. I _____ go, because _____ old servant Gabelle _____ my help. When _____ read this, I _____ be on my way. I did _____ tell you before _____ I knew you _____ worry. I promise I will _____ to you when I _____ to let you know I am _____.

    Take _____ of yourself and little Lucie and _____ father.

      Your loving _____, Charles

7 Is *A Tale of Two Cities* a good title for this story? Here are some other possible titles. Which do you like best, and why? What other titles can you think of?

| | |
|---|---|
| Revolution in France | Charles and Lucie |
| To the Guillotine! | Dying for Love |
| Blood and Tears | The Shadow of the Bastille |
| A City of Terror | Enemies of France |

8 Do you agree (A) or disagree (D) with these sentences? Explain why.

1 The Revolution was good for France in the end.
2 Madame Defarge was right to want revenge for what had been done to her family.
3 Sydney Carton was a better man than Charles Darnay.
4 Love is the strongest power in the world.

# ABOUT THE AUTHOR

Charles John Huffam Dickens (1812—70) was born in Portsmouth, in England. His family was extremely poor. The worst time for Dickens was when his father was sent to prison because he owed so much money, and Dickens himself was sent, aged only 12, to work in a factory. He remembered this terrible time all his life, and later wrote about it in his novel *David Copperfield* (1850). He then worked as a newspaper reporter and wrote his first novel, *The Pickwick Papers* (1837), which was very popular. In the next four years, he wrote *Oliver Twist* and two more novels, which were all very successful. He was now a well-known writer, whose stories, like *A Christmas Carol*, appeared in monthly magazines. In *A Tale of Two Cities* (1859), he showed his great interest in history, and in *Great Expectations* (1861) he wrote about the differences between the rich and the poor, which he had experienced himself in his own early life.

Although Dickens spent many hours a day writing, he also had time for his large circle of family and friends, writing for magazines, and for helping people in trouble. He felt strongly that everybody should be able to live in freedom. As he grew older, he worked harder than ever, continuing to write, and giving public readings of his works in Britain and America.

There have been hundreds of books, films, and plays about Dickens' stories. He is often called the greatest English novelist of all time, and his characters and their sayings have become so real to us that they are now part of our language and part of our everyday life.

# OXFORD BOOKWORMS LIBRARY

*Classics • Crime & Mystery • Factfiles • Fantasy & Horror*
*Human Interest • Playscripts • Thriller & Adventure*
*True Stories • World Stories*

The OXFORD BOOKWORMS LIBRARY provides enjoyable reading in English, with a wide range of classic and modern fiction, non-fiction, and plays. It includes original and adapted texts in seven carefully graded language stages which take learners from beginner to advanced level.

All Stage 1 titles, as well as over eighty other titles from Starter to Stage 6, are available as audio recordings. All Starters and many titles at Stages 1 to 4 are specially recommended for younger learners. Every Bookworm is illustrated, and Starters and Factfiles have full-color illustrations.

The OXFORD BOOKWORMS LIBRARY also offers extensive support. Each book contains an introduction to the story, notes about the author, a glossary, and activities. Additional resources include tests and worksheets, as well as answers for these and for the activities in the books. There is advice on running a class library, using audio recordings, and the many ways of using Oxford Bookworms in reading programs. Resource materials are available on the website <www.oup.com/elt/gradedreaders>.

The *Oxford Bookworms Collection* is a series for advanced learners. It consists of volumes of short stories by well-known authors, both classic and modern. Texts are not abridged or adapted in any way, but carefully selected to be accessible to the advanced student.

---

You can find details and a full list of titles in the *Oxford Bookworms Library Catalog* and *Oxford English Language Teaching Catalogs*, and on the website <www.oup.com/elt/gradedreaders>.

# Little Women

## LOUISA MAY ALCOTT

*Retold by John Escott*

When Christmas comes for the four March girls, there is no money for expensive presents, and they give away their Christmas breakfast to a poor family. But there are no happier girls in America than Meg, Jo, Beth, and Amy. They miss their father, of course, who is away at the Civil War, but they try hard to be good so that he will be proud of his "little women" when he comes home.

This heart-warming story of family life has been popular for more than a hundred years.

# Treasure Island

## ROBERT LOUIS STEVENSON

*Retold by John Escott*

"Suddenly, there was a high voice screaming in the darkness: 'Pieces of eight! Pieces of eight! Pieces of eight!' It was Long John Silver's parrot, Captain Flint! I turned to run …"

But young Jim Hawkins does not escape from the pirates this time. Will he and his friends find the treasure before the pirates do? Will they escape from the island and sail back to England with a ship full of gold?

# Dr. Jekyll and Mr. Hyde

## ROBERT LOUIS STEVENSON

*Retold by Rosemary Border*

You are walking through the streets of London. It is getting dark, and you want to get home quickly. You enter a narrow side-street. Everything is quiet, but as you pass the door of a large windowless building, you hear a key turning in the lock. A man comes out and looks at you. You have never seen him before, but you realize immediately that he hates you. You are shocked to discover, also, that you hate him.

Who is this man that everybody hates? And why is he coming out of the laboratory of the very respectable Dr. Jekyll?

# Wuthering Heights

## EMILY BRONTË

*Retold by Clare West*

The wind is strong on the Yorkshire moors. There are few trees and fewer houses to block its path. There is one house, however, that does not hide from the wind. It stands out from the hill and challenges the wind to do its worst. The house is called Wuthering Heights.

When Mr. Earnshaw brings a strange, small, dark child back home to Wuthering Heights, it seems he has opened his doors to trouble. He has invited in something that, like the wind, is safer kept out of the house.

# Great Expectations

## CHARLES DICKENS

*Retold by Clare West*

In a gloomy, neglected house Miss Havisham sits—as she has sat year after year—in a wedding dress and veil that were once white and are now faded and yellow with age. Her face is like a death's head; her dark eyes burn with bitterness and hate. By her side sits a proud and beautiful girl, and in front of her, trembling with fear in his thick country boots, stands young Pip.

Miss Havisham stares at Pip coldly and murmurs to the girl at her side, "Break his heart, Estella. Break his heart!"

# Pride and Prejudice

## JANE AUSTEN

*Retold by Clare West*

"The moment I first met you, I noticed your pride, your sense of superiority, and your selfish disdain for the feelings of others. You are the last man in the world whom I could ever be persuaded to marry," said Elizabeth Bennet.

And so Elizabeth rejects the proud Mr. Darcy. Can nothing overcome her prejudice against him? And what of the other Bennet girls—their fortunes and misfortunes in the business of getting husbands?

This famous novel by Jane Austen is full of wise and humorous observation of the people and manners of her times.